D0163064

What the Kite Thinks

a linked poem by

WING TEK LUM

JOSEPH STANTON

JEAN YAMASAKI TOYAMA

edited by Lucy Lower

SUMMER SESSION
UNIVERSITY OF HAWAI'I AT MĀNOA

©1994 by the
University of Hawai'i at Mānoa
Summer Session.

Manufactured in the
United States.

English translation of "What
the Kite Thinks" used by
permission of William I. Elliott,
Kawamura Kazuo, and
Jitsugetsu-kan.

ISBN 0–8248–1599–8

This book is printed on acid-
free paper and meets the
guidelines for permanence and
durability of the Council on
Library Resources.

Book design and cover by
Natalie M. Lee

Distributed by
University of Hawaii Press
Order Department
2840 Kolowalu Street
Honolulu, Hawai'i 96822

Contents

v

Preface

I think this poem and the process that produced it came as a bit of a surprise — profoundly enriching, maybe also a little sobering — to everyone connected with it. A collaboration of this sort is like a musical improvisation; it may, or may not, ever really take flight. There is no one controlling hand on the entire poem, and whether the separate links come together to make a poem and what kind of poem they do make is unimaginable until the last word is on the page. An important difference however is that collaborative improvisation is accepted musical practice and, accordingly, a skill cultivated by many musicians; poetic collaboration, aside from translation, is rare.

As was sometimes true in the joint composition of the poem itself, the idea for this experiment sprang from happy chance: an offhand remark by Victor Kobayashi, Dean of the Summer Session of the University of Hawaiʻi at Mānoa, passed on to me by Jean Toyama. Peter Tanaka, Director of International Programs for the Summer Session, and I had been exploring possible formats for a program in multi-lingual poetry, planned as one of several programs centering around the summer 1991 visit of Japanese poet Makoto Ōoka, whose efforts on behalf of international poetic communication are well known. Following Victor's suggestion, the decision was made to make a poem and not simply to talk about it.

We hoped to involve Hawaiʻi poets with a variety of voices for this unorthodox and somewhat daunting project, and Jean, Wing Tek Lum, and Joseph Stanton were game. Since they would have only the few days of Makoto's visit to work together face to face, they agreed to begin with a long distance round of poems beforehand. Thus when Makoto arrived on July 29th, he brought with him the fifth link. The next two days saw an explosive acceleration in composition, punctuated by two afternoon sessions in which the poets met together to take turns adding their poems, which by Friday, August 2nd, numbered sixteen.

The process itself of exchange, collaboration, communication, was central to the purpose of this program. Thus the afternoon sessions were open to interested observers, several of whom were stimulated to ancillary composition. Moreover, on that final Friday, the poets gave a public reading of the first sixteen links and commented on their experience; the commentary appended here is largely based on a transcript of that discussion. It is hoped that the commentary will not only provide insights into the poetic practices and values of these particular poets but will convey a sense of the possibilities that the linked poetry method may open up for experimentation, learning, and growth, both poetic and personal.

The focus and momentum of those few days was sufficiently compelling for the poets to decide to continue the poem, and over the next nine months links were added, by long distance again, until an agreed-upon total of thirty-six was achieved. The final product of this endeavor, the poem itself, strikes the essential balance aspired to in a traditional linked poem: it has shape as a whole, in the interplay of its several voices and in its overall trajectory, while each link yet retains its autonomy; and it is at once accessible to a wide readership and profoundly rooted in its time and place.

I would like to express my appreciation to the co-sponsors of this poetic experiment, the Center for Japanese Studies and the Summer Session, both of the University of Hawai'i at Mānoa, for their support. Additional funding was provided by the Hawai'i State Foundation on Culture and the Arts, the University of

Hawai'i Japan Studies Endowment, and the Hawai'i Literary Arts Council. Special thanks is due Dean Victor Kobayashi, and Mitsuru Andō and Shūji Takeuchi, Director and Editor, respectively, of *Bungei Shunjū,* for originally conceiving the project; and Peter Tanaka and his Summer Session staff for the enthusiasm and the organizational support that made its execution possible. Warmest thanks too to Hawai'i poet Tony Quagliano, our moderator for the public presentation of the first part of the poem, for his lively contributions to the event.

LUCY LOWER

What the Kite Thinks

Introduction

by Makoto Ōoka

Renshi, a linked poem by several poets, is a new free verse form of collaborative poetry adapted from the *renga* and *renku* forms favored by many classical poets in Japan since the thirteenth century. I began writing it in the 1970s with my fellow poets from the poetry magazine *Oars* (*Kai*). We met frequently in Tokyo from 1971 to compose linked poems, which were later collected in the volume *Oars: Linked Poetry* (1979).

Afterward, I spent the fall and winter of 1981 as poet-in-residence at Oakland University in Michigan. Poet Thomas Fitzsimmons is an old friend of mine who was then an English professor there. One evening in the course of conversation after dinner, he and I came up with the idea of composing a linked poem of twenty links in English. What attracted Thomas about linked poetry was the way it differed from the Western method of poetry writing, which seemed unable to free itself from the concept of the solitary creative act performed in self-important seclusion. Thomas and I did indeed compose our linked poem, and that was my first experience composing linked poetry on an international level.

In recent years there has been growing interest in linked verse in Europe as well. To date I have made linked poems more than ten times, with poets who write in as many languages, in locations as far flung as Berlin, Rotterdam, Paris, Helsinki, Frankfort, Lahti (Finland), and Tokyo. Sometimes we work in English, sometimes with excellent translators. Several of these efforts have been published: two volumes in German, one in Dutch, one in Finnish and one in Estonian. However, this volume of linked verse from Hawai'i seems to me perhaps the richest in content, and the most likely to provide the reader with a sense of just what linked poetry is and what possibilities experimentation with it might reveal.

In the classical *renga* and *renku* forms, three, four, or five poets would gather in a room and, following a minutely detailed set of rules, compose a poem of a predetermined number of alternating short and long links. Even the "long" link was only seventeen syllables, the same number as a haiku. From the seventeenth century on, the preferred length, the *kasen keishiki*, was a total of thirty-six of these short and long links. If three poets were to compose a *kasen keishiki*, then, each poet's contribution would consist of twelve links.

The rules that governed this classical form were rigorously detailed, and each poet sought to demonstrate his individual talent within these limitations—or rather, by making use of them. The rules of classical *renga* and *renku* were based on the peculiarities of the Japanese language itself and were conceived in intimate connection to Japanese manners and customs, and to natural surroundings; some of them are of an extremely refined complexity. Thus it is not possible to apply them to another language. Indeed, even were it possible to apply them to another language the effect would be unnatural and uncomfortable, because such reverence for rigid and formalistic rules, which in the past functioned as a springboard allowing the spirit free flight, has in the modern age become, on the contrary, a despotic spell impeding the movement of the spirit.

I feel that the important thing is to make the fundamental concept of *renga* and *renku* a creative premise for poetry now and in the future. In that sense the most valuable goal to be realized in making a linked poem on an international level is something like this: that several poets from different cultures, with different individual characters, join together with curiosity, sincerity, friendship, wit, and humor to engage in a process of mutual discovery which is difficult to pursue if not through the linked verse form. The result for the participating poets is the realization of an intimate and

2

creative dialogue, via the links of the poem itself, of a sort that is available nowhere else.

This cooperative enterprise can have the character of a kind of competition, even of confrontation, but this competition or confrontation is by no means personal. Rather, individual claims must be based on the principle that one gets the best from one's colleagues by offering one's own best effort. Indeed, the most notable principle of linked poetry is that since each of the poets is not simply composing a poem but is engaged in a mutual exchange—providing a poem to another and being provided by another with a poem—arbitrary egotistical demands could only have the most negative effect.

Poets who are unknown, even foreigners, to each other at the outset of such a collaborative work come to experience a kind of awakening in the course of joining together and composing their oeuvre. Each of us ends up revealing, to some degree, the secrets of his or her own creative process. And each gets a glimpse into the secrets of the others. In this way each participant's consciousness of life, his or her sense of reality, view of the world, even individual tendencies and tastes in expressive technique, become apparent. That experience alone is profoundly thrilling and moving.

In this atmosphere of friendly cooperation, the poets can come to understand in the deepest recesses of their hearts what another's laugh means, or a silence. In the same hypersensitive way that iron filings on a sheet of paper react to a magnet held underneath by forming a beautiful line, so a similar sensitivity vibrates in the heart of each poet in the composition of linked poetry.

Thus although we were actually together composing for only two or three days, we who were previously strangers became close friends. Even when making linked poetry with someone one already knows, one discovers superb new qualities in that person's talent. The fact that aspects of another's genius and individuality are so different from one's own surprises each of us, and that surprise gives rise to a real joy. In that joy is a recognition of the world's great diversity. And this recognition can be a first step in countering the progressive standardization, the disempowerment of individuals, that is eating away at the spiritual state of the modern world. We may even say that it is proof of the freedom of the spirit.

In the contemporary world, despite the phenomenal development of our "information culture," profound misunderstanding, misinterpretation, and conflict have actually intensified among different peoples, among different religions, and among cultures at different stages of development. Unfortunately, oppositions and differences of this scope cannot be easily resolved. In many places around the world, the late twentieth century is witnessing a widening of bloody suppression and wars of annihilation, all in the name of "resolving" such oppositions and differences. But does not our own future and that of the earth require a recognition of those oppositions and differences as evidence of our diversity, rather than as something to be dissipated by force? Does not our own future and that of the earth require mutual respect, even love, through development of our understanding of those very differences? For those of us who feel this way, linked poetry takes on symbolic meaning as a form of mutual understanding and exchange. This is because it is a form in which the participants treat each other's distinct personalities with the highest respect on the one hand, while on the other they seek to maintain a dynamic harmony.

Composing linked poetry in collaboration with Joseph Stanton, Jean Toyama and Wing Tek Lum, beginning in Hawai'i in the summer of 1991 and continuing by fax after my return to Japan until we had at last completed our sequence of thirty-six poems, has brought me feelings of great joy and pride. I feel a closeness to these three American poets that belies the fact that we actually sat at a table together for a mere two days. They feel the same toward me. It was indeed a marvelous experience. My memories of reading our linked poem and discussing our individual experience of it before a large audience at Jefferson Hall three days after we had first met, and the warmth, the curiosity, the sense of intimacy with the audience itself, are indelibly beautiful. The University of Hawai'i Summer Session, in carrying out this linked verse program, has contributed greatly to proving that contemporary poetry is not solely the low murmur of a solitary spirit. As a participant in the program, I would like to express my deep appreciation to all concerned with it at the University of Hawai'i.

MAKOTO ŌOKA

1. What the Kite Thinks

Because a hand holds me down to earth
I can climb the staircase of the sky.

Each time I push against the wind with my shoulders
I am sucked ever farther upward into the bosom of the sky.

Because a hand holds me down to earth
I hold the earth suspended in the air.

ŌOKA

2. *In the Air*

In the air rise the curlicues of incense
to pierce my nostrils
with the sense of the eternal
that I exhale in turn
to mingle with the here and now
of earthbound scents

TOYAMA

3. *Earthbound Scents*

Even the steam of evening coffee,
scented macadamia macaroon;
even the new-mown grass;
even the backyard sweet trajectories of white ginger
cannot distract us

from the new moon's narrow saxophone,
jamming with an all-star quartet—
blue notes floating down,
aromatic,
in the spaces between.

STANTON

4. *As She Sleeps on Her Stomach*

The spaces between her toes, her armpit,
the scoop of her shoulder where it hugs her neck,
the widening cleft where her thighs part her rump,
the triangle formed by one crooked elbow,
the hint of another by her bent knee,
the darkening shadow of her curved waist
suggesting the hollow beneath her belly
—these are the spaces that penetrate and define her,
these are the spaces of my love.

LUM

5. *The Spaces of My Love*

In the eastern sky clouds line up sunburnt.
On the desk in my studio
a man of obscure identity
rises out of a page of the world atlas
and along a river of female name
towards the voices of birds
he starts to build bridge after bridge.

ŌOKA

6. *Bridge After Bridge*

Don't cross them, she said, this place hides no treasures
no crystal forests or lapis rivers
no rose-petalled evenings
just an expanse of nothing—
that's all.

Don't let greedy curiosity get the best of you.
Obstacles are not always the promise of a prize.

TOYAMA

7. *The Promise of a Prize*

There are moments so ripe with promise—
cool air alive with cries of birds,
a glamour of gold sunsetting on a pond—
that we think the poems could write themselves,
and we hold to heart an unwon prize
that might not be a lie.

But last night the moon was so full
I could make nothing of it.

STANTON

8. *The Muse's Heart*

Nothing of it can be seen by the curious birds
their sight obscured by the sun's glitter
as if her eyes are no more than an expanse of mirrors
reflecting their own cruel lies.

But her hidden heart rises and falls
just as the belly of the ocean surges with the moon
her eyes sparkling from a phosphorescence within
a night beacon casting light and shadow for us all.

LUM

9. *Shadow for Us All*

On the bright theater stage
before the background panel
of evergreen pines
the Noh actor stands
a shadow woman's agonizing soul.

Although immobile, his hands move quickly
and wipe away—after three hours—
to the last drop the tears of blood
she has been shedding for over five centuries.

ŌOKA

10. *Over Five Centuries*

It took so long that the Venus de Milo grew arms
as big as Charles Atlas who carried the world
on his shoulders so no one would kick sand
in his face.

It took so long that the great wall of China
turned to dust that fills this hourglass
which I hold in my palm
counting the grains
bearing the load
wiping the tears from my eyes.

TOYAMA

11. *Wiping the Tears From My Eyes*

Under beads of dew in tall grass a cricket cries:
The abandoned daughter
sings her elegant, selfish lover
over treacherous midnight, or tries,
for all the good it does her.

She would cleanse her eyes in moonlight,
but the water rippling in the well
unravels her face until
it is only his.

STANTON

12. *It is Only His*

It is only his to choose
what pipe to smoke, what book to read,
what fish to steam and eat,
what sweater to put on, what ripened fruit to pick.
But he who gave us life calls us to his bedside
to say it must now be ours.
But it is only his to choose, this choice of death.

LUM

13. *This Choice of Death*

The most amazing thing I witnessed
in the aquarium at Waikīkī:
A video scene showing
the scorpionfish swallow his prey
so quickly that the action moved
from life to death without any sense of danger.
A fascinating sight proving
there is no evident boundary
between twilight and darkness
between inside and outside.

ŌOKA

14. *Inside and Outside*

both
from
no
just
only
grammatical bric-à-brac
defining
my I am

TOYAMA

15. *I Am*

I think therefore
I think
I am
thinking
these words.

Part of me is writing,
while the rest of me is watching
without giving any of this a second thought.

Most of me is now
watching you
and wondering
who you think you are.

STANTON

16. *Who You Think You Are*

The arrow smugly notes how straight she flies,
the hardness of her tip, how she whistles swiftly through the air.

The bow exults in how far back he can bend,
his tight, sinewy string, the deep resonance of his twang.

The target calls attention to the bright colors of his rings,
how solidly he stands, how he guides the arrow to his bull's-eye.

LUM

17. *His Bull's-Eye*

He hung in his bull's-eye center
the heart of his beloved, yearned for for ages:
when finally he hit the mark
his hands held only a woman's bloodless heart.

He hung in his bull's-eye center
the word SUCCESS in capital letters:
when at last he hit the mark
his hands held only his own bloodless heart.

ŌOKA

18. *Bloodless Heart*

Not in the face of bold adversaries
but early, before the birds' song,
it creeps away in silence and in calm.
Too soon beckoned from my sleep
I hear its retreating beat
and feel
once more its evaporation.
If standing I would quake,
but sleep—thank God—returns
as does it, when amid morning
chirps I find again my courage to begin.

TOYAMA

19. *To Begin*

Arriving in a strange city,
where I was once a child,
I meet the first crocuses of spring—
fierce salvos of color fired through
pale ironies of melting snow.

As I imagine the flowers unfolding,
faces from childhood unexpectedly
come to mind. Dead, almost-forgotten
eyes gaze intently into mine,
as if for the first time.

STANTON

20. *The First Time*

He does not remember the first time
he dared to hold her hand
or waited worried sick for her to call
or quarrelled and then made up without regrets
or sang duets or shared the dishwashing.
The moments that he cherishes
have nothing to do with their past.
Instead each morning they wake up face to face
as if for the first time, as if forever.

LUM

21. *As if Forever*

As if forever
a woman cherishes ice cream on her lips,
a boy plays with life in his poems,
and death is polishing in his hands
beautiful newborn human bodies.

Though the dust-filled blue sky
shines far away as if forever,
the Earth suddenly
becomes a big hole
at my back.

ŌOKA

22. *At My Back*

It howls there like some
wolf on my tail
famished by a long
season of want
spitting out crushed branches—
it dreams my bones instead.

If I slept, it would be on me
feasting on *my* dreams
getting its fill.

TOYAMA

23. *Getting Its Fill*

The silhouetted house,
worn paper thin by too much recollection,
has had its fill of the evening's
excess of shadows and broken stars.
Upright with disbelief, it raises
bare trees in front of its face,
as if to say, "No, not that . . .
anything but that!"

STANTON

24. *Anything But That*

The rains never stop, the land floods.
The night slugs seek out my house,
climb the high ground of my loft
to encircle my bed. I awaken
to their slick slime embalming me,
my ankles and thighs glued together in a sheen,
my arms, my jaw, my eyelids immobilized by ooze.
Their heavy, sleek bodies pry open my mouth
depositing their glistening young down my throat
before they curl up all around me
as we wait for the clear dawn.

LUM

25. *As We Wait for the Clear Dawn*

And finally when we opened the small window
we saw our ship, of cubic shape,
feebly hanging between rocks on the mountain.
The mud stuck on the tiny leaves
of a twig brought back by my dove
had already dried to powder.
My 601st springtime was to start on this powder.
Though no one in the ship knew
how, on this boundless expanse of water,
the brilliant summer would surely come, or fail to,
after this strange dawn of spring
—my family, every pair of animals, birds,
cows, hens, and snakes,
all ignorant without exception.

ŌOKA

26. *Ignorant Without Exception*

It was a good little war,
a short and sweet little war,
a splendid little war.

It brought us together,
made us feel proud,
made us feel strong and good,
like we thought we felt before.

So when we feel out of touch,
out of sorts, full of nasty warts,
we'll start a little war,
a sweet little war,
a splendid little war.

TOYAMA

27. *A Little War*

He is almost lost somewhere outdoors
inside himself—
that fanatic boy, pounding the worn ball
against the shoveled backyard in the dead
cold of winter, late into the night with only
a streetlight to see by, at war with himself
over what he might or might not be,
throwing again and again
at a goal he cannot see;
somewhere in the dark
the war goes on and on
and will not be lost
and will not be won.

STANTON

28. *The Day will Not be Won*

The day will not be won
without the lover's kiss on parting
the foreman's praise on a job well done
the doctor's beaming smile in the delivery room
a mother's hug, a teammate's buttocks pat
a nod of understanding from a teacher
the applause of listeners at a rally
the wink of a child's mischievous eye
as all around us the desolate night descends.

LUM

29. *As All Around Us the Desolate Night Descends*

Eyes!
Take in the birds!
Take in the woods!
Take in the stars!

Turn all these
into sensuous foods.

And you, poet's hands!
Preserve in secret in your sinews
the silence that ensues

when the woods under the stars have disappeared,
and the birds, under the cover of the trees.

ŌOKA

30. *Under the Cover of Trees*

Maybe peaches weren't meant to be this good
devoured beneath heavy branches
exuding the suave fragrance of
uncanny blossoms.

But sinking our hungry teeth
into lush flesh, the juices
flowing from our sated lips,
we thank the trees for their gifts.

TOYAMA

31. *We Thank the Trees for Their Gifts*

Lavender bells that ring down only as color
become a place in the road to look for,
day after day for the month it takes
the wind to bring all the flowers down.

One month of jacaranda rain
and my mind turns lavender,
lilac feathers falling and falling,
pieces of sky whose blue has pinked
to lavender, that unearthly color,
unreality become lovely,
what every dream should be.

STANTON

32. *What Every Dream Should be*

Take a freshly-laid egg, a lock of hair,
a hangman's noose, the nose of a moose,
a mare's breath after her canter,
a floppy disk, an aria and ceramic tile and a python snake,
last month's banana leaf,
the curve of his waist and a grandmother's caress
—place them all in my daughter's book bag to shake,
then piece by piece pull each out
tossing one and all into the clear, white midnight air.

LUM

33. *The Clear, White Midnight Air*

Let's toast the last cup of saké
under this ripened moon of May.
A good saké turns into
a stream of Time
on our softened tongues,
and passes along our throats
to melt into everyone's ocean inside.
After a while it returns, our good saké,
from a long way off,
changing into a phrase of melody,
faint, but still audible.

ŌOKA

34. Faint, but Still Audible

That hum within my head, some strain
long forgotten, grooved along
my limbic convolutions
turns electric and flashes
over spaces, over time.

The one that you inscribed
still alive, still pulsing
turns notes into cadenza,
accidents into life.

TOYAMA

35. *Accidents into Life*

We have gone out on this limb
of thirty-six twists and turns of phrase,
fearful that we would fall
or be left suspended in our animation—
like the cartoon branch that keeps Bugs Bunny in mid-air,
while Elmer, saw in hand, and the rest of the world
fall impossibly away;
but—even when the world falls away—
the writing must go on, somehow,
a bridge we build in front of us, and behind,
one step at a time.

STANTON

36. *One Step at a Time*

One step at a time over a gully
across a rope bridge of words.
No matter that I cannot soar
into these blank white clouds
like the gawking birds overhead.
My three friends here float me up
as I sway about these high wire days
readying my prance,
my dark hula, my pirouette.

L U M

Commentary by the Poets

[The following remarks are based on a transcript of the public presentation of the first sixteen links of the poem on August 2, 1991. —Ed.]

MAKOTO ŌOKA: First of all, I wish to express my great respect for and gratitude to the Summer Session program of this university. Thanks to this program, I was able to come here and work together with these three really fine poets of Hawai'i. Today we will read our collective poem, most of which we composed in the last two days. This kind of poem is called *renshi* in Japanese; in English, linked poems. So far we have made sixteen links. The concept of the *renshi* or linked poems might seem strange to you because people tend to think that poets write their poems in seclusion, quite the contrary of what we have been doing. Most contemporary poetry is conceived and written by poets living in some manner of seclusion. But in Japanese tradition there has long been another way of making poetry—that is, making poetry collectively—which gave birth to such fine poets as the great Matsuo Bashō of the seventeenth century.

Bashō was undoubtedly Japan's finest haiku poet. But I think one cannot understand him thoroughly without knowing the works he produced in collaboration with his ardent followers. He never wished to publish collections of his own poetry; instead he was very eager to make collections of the poetry of his group, unquestionably of the highest quality in the history of Japanese poetry. I think his attitude represents the most essential way of thinking of poets in the Japanese tradition. Poems, far from being expressions of individual genius, were rather a form of witty and generous conversation between spirits who shared a respect for each other's unique individuality.

Thus a tradition of forming some sort of "poetic banquet" became the mainstream of Japanese classical poetry. *Renga* or *renku,* both meaning "linked poetry," was the natural outcome. I myself was inspired to remake this classical form into a new version for contemporary poets, not only Japanese but from any language or nation. I called this new version *renshi*, still meaning "linked poetry," but of contemporary free verse.

An exciting experience for me came in 1981 when I made a linked poem with an American poet, a longtime friend of mine, Thomas Fitzsimmons. He was at that time a professor of English at Oakland University in Michigan, where I stayed for three months as poet-in-residence. We talked often about poetry. One evening we were chatting about traditional Japanese poetry and when I spoke of the spirit of collaboration I have been describing to you here, he seemed surprised and at the same time deeply interested. And he proposed that we make a collaborative poem ourselves, then and there. I was rather doubtful about what the result would be, but anyway we began on that evening. I translated a short poem of mine into English, and he made the second poem and I made the third and so on. Thus we continued until we had twenty poems.

Quite by accident I adopted a form of linking in which a poet takes the last line or last word of the previous poem written by another as the title of his own poem. In thus capping the previous poem, the poet has some sense of continuity or of expanding or developing its ideas, but in a very different direction. I thought this form of making collective poetry was very productive, and so here I proposed to make the same sort of collective work and my three colleagues have been, I think, very pleased with this idea too. So this is the second time I have made this type of linked poem.

I have made somewhat similar linked poems on more than ten other occasions in collaboration with French, English, Dutch, German, Estonian, Finnish, and Peruvian poets in several places in Europe: Berlin, Paris, Rotterdam, Helsinki. This June I went to Lahti in Finland where two Finnish poets, one Estonian poet, and I made a linked poem of thirty-six rather short verses. One of the

Finnish poets wrote in Finnish but the other wrote in Swedish, so the whole poem was in four languages. Two of the others were adept in English and they immediately translated our poems into English. We gave an evening reading in a municipal library; each of us read in his own language and the English translation for all thirty-six poems was read by Canadian poet Richard Lemm. It was an event in an international festival of writers. The audience was enthusiastic and I am sure you will be intrigued here also by the works of my three colleagues.

I have embraced this type of collaboration because I have felt that the long years of poets' seclusion have lost them many readers. I think such seclusion is an international phenomenon. There has been a sense among poets themselves of the loss of meaningful human contact, and at the same time the decline in readership has become obvious. In making linked poems one must necessarily "connect" with the other poets. When I write a poem, the other three poets give me good advice on the spot, or they might criticize the poem's flaws, or simply point out a misspelling—something like that. So the writing inevitably has a collective aspect, reflecting the direct appreciation or criticism of others. And when I finish my poem the next poet is in turn the object of criticism or appreciation. This has a very good and refreshing effect on oneself. Thus deeply involved, we become very close friends because we create something new together, especially something new to ourselves. Finally, I am convinced that to create something together is worth trying in this *fin de siècle* atmosphere. I have talked too much, so I give my place to Jean. Thank you.

JEAN YAMASAKI TOYAMA: Writing collaboratively has been a wonderful experience. Until a few weeks ago I was the kind of poet Makoto described. Alone. In seclusion. If I wrote, it was by accident. Only when the spirit moved me; when she didn't move, neither did I. So my thirty years of writing has really been a dribble.

One year when I won a minor writing prize I was asked how I would describe myself as a writer. I said I guess I would call myself a "closet poet." It wasn't so much that I was ashamed of being a poet, it was that I didn't really think that I was a poet. Yesterday my husband said "you must be a poet," because I was running around gleefully waiting for the next poem. And I agreed, I must be a poet.

Rather than a solitary act, writing *renshi* is a communal one. We will be talking individually about the links that we've written, but I would like to describe in general how this has evolved for me over the few weeks we have been working. In the beginning I was very concerned about the reaction of my fellow poets, their criticism. I really didn't want the immediate feedback. I thought I would rather have a letter of rejection come anonymously through the mail. [Laughter] There are a lot of poets out there. And so it was kind of scary. On my first turn I wrote two links—just in case the first one didn't pass muster. And then, I wanted to make it easy for the next person. But as time went on, I wanted to make it harder.

JOSEPH STANTON: I know exactly what Jean is saying about the difficulty of the *renshi* process. When I received her most recent link, I thought, "Now, how am I going to rise to this occasion!"

For me, a marvelous aspect of this activity is the way it makes poetry writing a necessity. You know you have to write, and you know you have to do it right now and in accordance with a set of rules and expectations. Both the necessity and the constraints are wonderfully liberating. We have imposed on ourselves a literary method that pushes aside the usual interferences that so often prevent us from writing on any given day. I don't know if it is just an American problem, but it has been my observation that for many poets, everything in life seems to conspire against the writing of poetry. All of our systems of obligation at home and work tacitly exclude poetry writing. In the scheme of things it seems an aberration to want to take the time to write a poem.

Poetry writing is an inner compulsion. Many of us cannot not write. It has to happen. It is inseparable from our sense of ourselves and our understanding of what it is to be alive, but since we are so often prevented from writing, it is marvelous to have an instance where we are assigned to write a brief poem within a limited time and with the expectation that we will accept a title arbitrarily assigned by the last line of the preceding poem. This *renshi*-writing activity is a rare instance where the inner compulsion to write poetry is supported by a structured procedure. Thus, the genuine difficulty of the *renshi*-writing discipline becomes a difficulty devoutly to be wished. The rules of the game—the need for brevity, the assignment of topic by the ending of the previous poem, the time limitations, and the desire to make individual parts satisfactory components of the whole—all are aids to composition as well as limitations.

As both Jean and Makoto have mentioned, the social nature of this activity is a special feature. In writing the *renshi* we are communicating with each other, but we are also working as a team to make something for the world in general. We have come together to form a small working group of dedicated individuals in order to achieve a single common goal within a limited amount of time.

It is exciting to have the opportunity to work with Ōoka Makoto in his ongoing international experimentation in linked-verse collaboration. By participating with him we are, in a sense, linking our *renshi* to all his other *renshi*, thus becoming part of what might be called a *renshi* of *renshi* where the leadership of Ōoka is what links all the collaborations together. Ōoka's importance as a poet and scholar in Japan adds an historical dimension to what we are attempting. Ōoka's involvement in the linked verse tradition connects his avant-garde international experiments, including the one he is involved in with us, to classical precedents.

The opportunity to work with Wing Tek Lum and Jean Toyama has also been greatly rewarding. Our shared assignment gives us a point of productive contact that enables us to enjoy sympathetic participation in each other's work. It is an unusual pleasure to be able to take pride in a great line written by another writer because it is part of a poem that belongs to all of us.

WING TEK LUM: I won't say too much more because I think my fellow poets have said enough. I think the main thing I have learned from this experience is that I found it was very difficult to write a poem. [Laughter] Especially because of the limitations of time—I had to get it back to the next person within a certain period of time. Also the space limitations, as we all agree that we are not writing epic poetry, but only six to eight lines. And third, the limitation on theme; one gets stuck with the title for one's poem because that's part of the rules, to use the last line of the previous poem. However, the main limitation was the limitation on ego, and that was something that was a bit risky. This is more of a cooperative effort, as my fellow writers have said, rather than simply the project of a closet writer fooling around on his own. I have written in another context that I am an epiphany writer, not the kind of person who keeps a journal or practices a lot. I write whenever the spirit moves me and that is very infrequently. And so this exercise was very important in the sense that it taught me how to write for deadlines with these other limitations. (Now, of course some people would say that even if I weren't operating within these limitations they wouldn't like my poems anyway. [Laughter]) I think it taught me a sense of spontaneity which I think is very important and I want to link that up with other kinds of creative efforts, such as Chinese calligraphy. The calligrapher practices every day, say in the morning for two hours. And yet he is called upon to write a memorial for somebody in an instant, and that memorial has to be beautifully done. Or the kung fu master who somehow gets attacked or mugged on the street. He practices every day for many hours and then one day gets mugged, and again it is a very spontaneous situation where he has to respond. I look at this kind of endeavor as practicing for getting mugged. [Laughter] I think that's all I have to say.

[The poem to that date, the first sixteen links, was read, and then each link was commented upon and read by its author as follows. —Ed.]

ŌOKA: Although I am now somewhat accustomed to making these things, I always feel some difficulty at the outset. Usually, I am asked to make the first poem because I am a little more trained than the others who are writing for the first time. This time, too, I was asked to write the first poem, but since in principle I cannot write a linked poem without the presence of the others, it was very hard for me to make a poem which would work to get us really launched. I proposed to Mr. Peter Tanaka, who organized this Summer Session program, that he might ask the other poets about starting with a poem of mine which has already been published. The poem, actually, is in *Elegy and Benediction*, published very recently in Tokyo, in connection with Katydid Books, and I had hoped it would already have arrived at the university bookstore. But the books had been dispatched in late June, so they are now still on the Pacific Ocean, very pacifically. [Laughter] Anyway, this poem, "What the Kite Thinks," is one of the poems included in that book. I was very relieved to know through Peter's fax that Jean had continued with her poem, "In the Air." I am always somewhat the slave of time while I am working in Tokyo and so I have been so sorry for my fellow poets. This poem was very short, so I thought it might be suitable for the first poem.

1. *What the Kite Thinks*

Because a hand holds me down to earth
I can climb the staircase of the sky.

Each time I push against the wind with my shoulders
I am sucked ever farther upward into the bosom of the sky.

Because a hand holds me down to earth
I hold the earth suspended in the air.

TOYAMA: We felt suspended in the air for quite a long time waiting for Makoto's poem to arrive. When it did, we didn't know who was to follow. After a few phone calls we decided that the first one finished would be the next in line. I lived and cooked and bathed "in the air," "in the air."

The first image that came in the air was scud missiles. The bombardment of Iraq was an eerie sight—terrifying and terrible, but a beautiful sight. I knew that poem was difficult, so I wrote another, inspired by the incense coming from the Kuan Yin Temple on Vineyard Boulevard. As soon as I got the first line, the rest just followed. I sent both to Joe and Wing Tek.

2. *In the Air*

In the air rise the curlicues of incense
to pierce my nostrils
with the sense of the eternal
that I exhale in turn
to mingle with the here and now
of earthbound scents

STANTON: As Jean mentioned, she gave me two poems from which to choose. I did not know her preference, so I decided to make things as easy for myself as possible by linking with the poem whose last line seemed most suggestive for me. I quickly decided that "earthbound scents" was an image that would be a workable starting point for me. Therefore, my choice between the two poems, which I felt were equally good, was entirely a practical and self-indulgent decision.

You may recall that there was a Saturday evening in early June [1991] when there was a visually spectacular coming together of heavenly bodies. Just above the western horizon several planets clustered close to each other and to the crescent moon. If I were to look up the exact date of that occurence, I could give you the exact date of the first draft of my first poem in this collaboration. I was delighted with the image that evening had given me, and I felt I had the poem well in hand. As it turned out, however, I had a hard time finishing the poem. I went through draft after draft without being really happy with the results. At that time I was teaching an intensive one-week creative writing workshop. The stimulation of that workshop may have contributed to my openness to images and my preoccupation with revision. I kept adding and subtracting images that related to earthbound scents and what I took to be the dreamlike reversal of those grounded aromas—"skybound" sights described as musical sounds. I really did smell new-mown grass that evening, but I threw in the white ginger and coffee aromas from my memory's stockpile of favorite scents that might have been smelled on such an evening. Macadamia macaroon is my favorite variety of flavored coffee, but I also chose that phrase for the chance it gave me to include a rhyme with *moon*. I have always felt that the *oo* sound can become magical when it is repeated. I wanted the evening evoked in the poem to sound magical because that is the way it felt.

3. *Earthbound Scents*

Even the steam of evening coffee,
scented macadamia macaroon;
even the new-mown grass;
even the backyard sweet trajectories of white ginger
cannot distract us

from the new moon's narrow saxophone,
jamming with an all-star quartet—
blue notes floating down,
aromatic,
in the spaces between

LUM: I had the enviable position of being clean-up hitter in the sense that I could get to see what everyone else was doing and I could procrastinate about my own creative effort. On the other hand, it was also rather intimidating because I saw what wonderful efforts were being made already. And I was especially stunned by Joe's image of the moon which I had also seen that same night, and I said to myself, "Wow, this is a great image. How am I going to top this one?" It took me a long time to write and I made a number of different starts on the poem which are totally unrelated to what is now on the printed page. It took me about a week; I took a long time to respond. I noticed that there were a lot of images about being "in between" in the first three poems: the kite and also the sense of time—a lot of things going back and forth. But I had got stuck with this stupid ending of "the spaces between." [Laughter] So I thought maybe I should do something differently and what triggered my poem was thinking about spaces between. I got hooked on "between her toes," and that's how the poem started. I would also like to say that I made an error in that I had misremembered the rules and took the last three or four words of the previous poem to start mine, rather than as its title. I wanted to point that out for both poems four and eight.

4. *As She Sleeps on Her Stomach*

The spaces between her toes, her armpit,
the scoop of her shoulder where it hugs her neck,
the widening cleft where her thighs part her rump,
the triangle formed by one crooked elbow,
the hint of another by her bent knee,
the darkening shadow of her curved waist
suggesting the hollow beneath her belly
—these are the spaces that penetrate and define her,
these are the spaces of my love.

ŌOKA: I was surprised to get such a quick response from these poets; my fax machine rang one evening with three poems. An attack! [Laughter] In some ways it was a good thing to be attacked and awaken, because I had a bad case of jet lag after travelling to Europe. Besides, I had so many things to do before I came to Hawai'i. Having a column in a big Japanese newspaper, the *Asahi*, each day I write a small commentary about a Japanese poem, ancient, modern, or contemporary. I've been doing it for twelve years. There can be no pause in that column—people are waiting for some beautiful, or comical, or heavy, profound poem, which many of them read there for the first time. Needless to say, it is something to read every morning—a poem and short commentary on it—on the front page of a major newspaper. So before I came to Hawai'i I had to write about twenty or thirty columns in advance. Very hard work. I also had other articles to write. Still, I always had in my mind "the spaces of my love," "the spaces of my love." [Laughter] Finally on the day before I was to leave Japan I decided to write "Spaces of My Love." It was already morning—I always work until morning—when I stood by my desk and had a vision of a human being standing there. It was me, possibly. But anyway I saw that vague presence. I decided to write about him. He should have some idea of love. Outside the birds were already singing busily and cheerfully, in contrast to my mind. I sat before the desk and I wrote this poem down very quickly. But of course I wrote in Japanese and so I had to translate it, postponing my getting into bed by two hours. Though the translation might be very bad, I hoped the other poets would be able to correct my poem—my spelling and my way of writing. That is the most important—the best—thing about making this sort of poem; someone can correct it. With that help, we can continue.

5. *The Spaces of My Love*

In the eastern sky clouds line up sunburnt.
On the desk in my studio
a man of obscure identity
rises out of a page of the world atlas
and along a river of female name
towards the voices of birds
he starts to build bridge after bridge.

TOYAMA: This poem came hot off the fax. Peter called me and dictated the poem over the phone. (As you can see, technology was an integral part of this ancient art.) I stared at the last three words, "bridge after bridge."

I said, well, let's think about the Japanese word for bridge. Then I thought I would pun with the word bridge. Bridge is such a simple word but it has many possibilities: a bridge on a violin or a bridge in music or a dental bridge. But I said, no, you cannot write about the dentist. Well, maybe I could have.

Somehow "bridge after bridge" gave me a feeling of too much harmony, too much goodness. Let's put in a minor chord, I thought.

I remembered a poem by Edna St. Vincent Millay that stuck in my head called "Bluebeard." In it her space has been invaded by an intruder. Once trespassed upon she must leave. I decided to write a cautionary tale about the dangers of building too many bridges. I also wanted to build a bridge with one of Makoto's poems in which he speaks of crystal forests.

6. *Bridge After Bridge*

Don't cross them, she said, this place hides no treasures
no crystal forests or lapis rivers
no rose-petalled evenings
just an expanse of nothing—
that's all.

Don't let greedy curiosity get the best of you.
Obstacles are not always the promise of a prize.

Here I am addressing myself; the poem both tempts and cautions. The challenge of an obstacle is sometimes irresistible, we think the prize is the goal when it shouldn't be.

STANTON: The phrase "the promise of a prize" immediately struck me as relevant to the trouble we had put upon ourselves by undertaking *renshi* writing, and in fact the phrase is descriptive of the whole difficult enterprise of poetry writing, where there is so often the *promise* of a prize that remains, or seems to remain, elusive. The phrase brought to mind the tantalizing nature of so many of my attempts to write poems. When I start to write I am always spurred on by the hope that I might be successful and somehow manage to actually capture something in words in a worthwhile way. In this poem I am trying to describe what that desire feels like. I am trying to write a poem about trying to write a poem. The effort is so often frustratingly tantalizing because what motivates the writer to continue is a glimmer of a notion of what might be possible if it all goes well. Too often the results do not quite live up to the writer's hope, thus making it seem that perhaps the original instinctive confidence in the possibility of success was unwarranted. Of course, success and adequacy in any form of art are not always easy to determine. There is always the chance that in some sense the poet has succeeded, has won some sort of "prize" of insight and form, even though what he has come up with is not quite what he had expected or thought he wanted. Thus I added "might not be a lie."

My use of *sunsetting* has multiple associations for me. This warping of sunset into a verb is an aberration that derives from bureaucratic jargon. It seems amusing, to me at least, to return the warped form of the word back to its original landscape context.

The statement I make in the last two lines of the poem has been rattling around in my head for almost twenty years now. [Laughter] It was wonderful to at last find a place where I could use it. That statement has always been my private way of saying to myself that there are things so wondrous we can never hope to capture them in words.

7. *The Promise of a Prize*

There are moments so ripe with promise—
cool air alive with cries of birds,
a glamour of gold sunsetting on a pond—
that we think the poems could write themselves,
and we hold to heart an unwon prize
that might not be a lie.

But last night the moon was so full
I could make nothing of it.

LUM: When I got this poem, again, it was a little bit intimidating. I could use "nothing of it." It didn't seem very promising. Again I point out that in error I didn't use it as the title. What I decided to do was to have a little bit of fun and steal words from the previous poems presented. And so I think for the first six or so lines there is at least one word that is stolen from a previous poem. I really didn't figure out what I was doing until the end of the first stanza. I was just fooling around with coming up with a couple of phrases, a couple of things to bring in. But I did home in on "expanse of mirrors," stealing it from an older poem of mine which has never been published, about someone looking into the eyes of another and seeing his reflection and that there can be danger in that. Then, later on, I wanted to kind of tie it in to Joe's theme of poetry and that is how the second stanza evolved. Originally, I didn't have the title, "The Muse's Heart." I changed it with the thought of linking it to Joe's poem about poetry.

8. *The Muse's Heart*

Nothing of it can be seen by the curious birds
their sight obscured by the sun's glitter
as if her eyes are no more than an expanse of mirrors
reflecting their own cruel lies.

But her hidden heart rises and falls
just as the belly of the ocean surges with the moon
her eyes sparkling from a phosphorescence within
a night beacon casting light and shadow for us all.

ŌOKA: "Shadow for us all"; that gives many images, of course, but I wanted to make something concrete rather than talk about some shadow more or less abstract. I have a weakness for thinking about things in the abstract, so I try to be concrete in my making of linked poems. Here, I finally thought about the shadow as a human being, but of course human beings are not naturally "shadows." In Japanese literary tradition, the shadow is very often a *spectre*, a ghost. Especially in the Noh theater, the actor embodies some ghost. And from a tactical viewpoint, it is very good for us Japanese to go back to Japanese tradition when making linked poems abroad. [Laughter] So I grasped the image of a Noh actor and made this poem. I also wanted to convey in this poem a sense of time.

9. *Shadow for Us All*

On the bright theater stage
before the background panel
of evergreen pines
the Noh actor stands
a shadow woman's agonizing soul.

Although immobile, his hands move quickly
and wipe away—after three hours—
to the last drop the tears of blood
she has been shedding for over five centuries.

TOYAMA: As we were leaving the workshop session, Makoto said we should be funny; we should have some humor in this poem because people like humor; they want to laugh. I don't usually write things that are funny, so I racked my brain trying to think what could be funny about "for over five centuries." [Laughter]

Since Makoto went back to his Japanese tradition, I went back to Western tradition and dug up the Venus de Milo. What can be funny about the Venus de Milo? Well, if she grew arms, she might be funny. But she would be funnier still if her arms were really big. I didn't think of [Arnold] Schwarzenegger. He's not of my generation, but I thought about Charles Atlas. As a kid I remember all those ads about growing muscles—they didn't call it pumping iron—and the importance of not being that puny weakling who got sand kicked in his face. So that's how this came about. I tried to stay funny, but somehow I ended up crying.

10. *Over Five Centuries*

It took so long that the Venus de Milo grew arms
as big as Charles Atlas who carried the world
on his shoulders so no one would kick sand
in his face.

It took so long that the great wall of China
turned to dust that fills this hourglass
which I hold in my palm
counting the grains
bearing the load
wiping the tears from my eyes.

STANTON: This time I was the one who ended up writing two poems—one inspired by thoughts about my father who died twenty-one years ago and the other inspired by a Noh play. For better or worse, I decided to use the Noh poem.

I have for a long time been preoccupied with Noh plays. After Makoto contributed "Shadow for Us All" to the *renshi*, I asked him what Noh play he had in mind as he was composing that poem. When I returned home that night I looked up the English translation of the play *Izutsu* ["The Well Curb"] and later decided that a poem inspired by that play could be one way to make the best of the line Jean had given me to work with as a title.

My poem tries to speak for and through the pathos of the all-consuming love that lies at the heart of Noh plays such as *Izutsu*. It would not be necessary, however, for the reader to know the plot of the play to read my poem. My goal in this piece is to get at the basic human dynamic of a brief but powerful dream narrative. The stance that underlies a poem of this kind involves a pretence that the play is somehow a dream that the speaker has dreamed; the poem is an attempt to capture the essence of the dream-play's action from the inside. Of course, no matter how hard I try to be true to my understanding of the Noh play I cannot escape the idiosyncracies that arise from my speaker's mind. My Noh poems inevitably take on lives of their own. They are haunted in more than one way.

11. *Wiping the Tears From My Eyes*

Under beads of dew in tall grass a cricket cries:
The abandoned daughter
sings her elegant, selfish lover
over treacherous midnight, or tries,
for all the good it does her.

She would cleanse her eyes in moonlight,
but the water rippling in the well
unravels her face until
it is only his.

LUM: "It is only his" was, I thought, relatively easy to follow compared to the other poems I had received before. I kept thinking about this particular phrase and the image I came up with was that of a pipe, for some reason. From there I developed a list and I formed that list around a person who would have a pipe, and that triggered some other kinds of memories. I don't know why it came into my consciousness, but my father also had a pipe, and he had died some time ago, and so I was thinking about that period of time when he was dying. Those kinds of memories came to mind, and so after I came up with this list I already knew what the ending was going to be. I had in fact told Joe during the period I was working on the poem that I already had the beginning and the ending but I was trying to figure out the middle part.

12. *It is Only His*

It is only his to choose
what pipe to smoke, what book to read,
what fish to steam and eat,
what sweater to put on, what ripened fruit to pick.
But he who gave us life calls us to his bedside
to say it must now be ours.
But it is only his to choose, this choice of death.

ŌOKA: "This choice of death"; it is rather difficult to write under this title. [Laughter] I took over an hour to think about it. This title immediately reminded me of the suicide of Mishima Yukio. But I hated to write about him in this linked poem—it is so sad. So I changed my mind. I thought about two or three other things. A voice within told me "always be concrete," and finally I remembered something I had seen at the Waikīkī Aquarium two or three days ago. I am very fond of the aquarium and the zoo. I went to the aquarium and I found many very beautiful fish, but the most interesting, or rather, shocking image was not in the glass tanks of the aquarium but on the video display. [Laughter] I am ashamed but I chose to write the poem from this source.

13. *This Choice of Death*

The most amazing thing I witnessed
in the aquarium at Waikīkī:
A video scene showing
the scorpionfish swallow his prey
so quickly that the action moved
from life to death without any sense of danger.
A fascinating sight proving
there is no evident boundary
between twilight and darkness
between inside and outside.

If you have not gone to the aquarium please do go there. There is a very shocking scene on the TV, I assure you. There had been a small fish just in front of the scorpionfish and the next moment, nothing. Even the action of biting was no action; at least, the scorpionfish always seemed to remain very still. In front of him—there was some smoke, that's all. [Laughter] It was amazing.

TOYAMA: We later found out that the proper setting for writing *renshi* is a room full of food and drink, preferably saké, wine, or beer. While enjoying each others' company and partaking of the banquet the poets would write in quick succession and try as much as possible to impede the progress of their partners.

Makoto never really explained this "impeding part" of writing. All this time we had actually tried to be cooperative and helpful. Since we now knew the other side of the game, our tactics changed. We told stories and jokes, trying to engage his attention.

But he was really concentrating and ignored us. At the same time Tony Quagliano challenged me: "Okay, Jean, you only have fifteen minutes to write yours."

We were nearing the end of the afternoon session, and Makoto was eating up all the time. Once I got the last line I decided to take up the challenge and give myself only five minutes, the time to walk to the parking lot. I knew I was not going to match Makoto's image of the scorpionfish, but I wanted to say the same thing that there is no boundary between inside and outside. So I decided to do just the opposite. Make it quick and simple.

It came to my head just as I approached my car: both inside and outside, from inside and outside, no inside and outside, just inside and outside, only inside and outside.

But I figured you already knew that was the way it was supposed to go, so I didn't need to write it that way.

14. *Inside and Outside*

> both
> from
> no
> just
> only
> grammatical bric-à-brac
> defining
> my I am

That last line gave me so much fun. You should have seen me yesterday as I was about to go out running. It was 6:15, and I was putting on my shoes. I just giggled and laughed, thinking about Joe. I had just read the poem to him over the phone. I thought, "What is he going to do with that last line? How is he going to eat his dinner?" Such a deliciously malicious feeling ran over me. Of course, it was an innocent maliciousness.

STANTON: I enjoyed the "innocent" (innocent as a scorpionfish?) joy with which Jean gave me this tough assignment. [Laughter] It had me stymied at first. How was I to write a poem with the title "My I Am"? I kept racking my brains. I thought at first that I would try something colloquial—something like "*My*, I am tired today." [Laughter] But I could not think of anything that could develop out of that. After considerable cogitation it occurred to me that I might have more luck if I just went with the last two words, "I am," as my title. My way was made clearer when I recalled a conversation I had had with Jean about the value of injecting humor into our sequence. I decided to try to write a funny poem in response to her funny poem. Since Jean is a scholar of French literature, I thought I might try to bring Descartes' famous line— "I think, therefore I am"—into my poem. I am not sure how well this works, but I had fun writing it.

It occurred to me after finishing this poem that this might be the first time I was giving Wing Tek a title that he would be happy to have.

15. *I Am*

I think therefore
I think
I am
thinking
these words.

Part of me is writing,
while the rest of me is watching
without giving any of this a second thought.

Most of me is now
watching you
and wondering
who you think you are.

LUM: Of course the "you" in Joe's poem is me. [Laughter] You know, I had seen a couple of earlier poems by my fellow writers talking about identity and I thought, "This should be easy. I have written on the subject before." And I was thinking that somehow this was linked to a poem which came to mind early, shortly after Joe had called. Last week I was talking to my niece about Arthur Sze, a poet that some of you know who lives in New Mexico, a Chinese American poet. And he has a famous poem called "Dazzled" that is about identity—actually, about reality. It describes the musings of individual musicians while they are playing in a chamber quartet. So I got that kind of idea from Arthur's poem. Somehow I figured I'd think about bows and arrows and things like that. And so I came up with this poem in that way. Perhaps others may disagree, but after I finished it I thought maybe it was fitting—my contribution in some small way to sum up this particular effort that we've made—in that writers are not persons whose identity or efforts are simply ours alone but that we are linked together, either directly through these linked poems or in other ways. That is what I think Arthur was saying in his poem, and I think that is what I tried to do in this one.

16. *Who You Think You Are*

The arrow smugly notes how straight she flies,
the hardness of her tip, how she whistles swiftly through the air.

The bow exults in how far back he can bend,
his tight, sinewy string, the deep resonance of his twang.

The target calls attention to the bright colors of his rings,
how solidly he stands, how he guides the arrow to his bull's-eye.

AFTERWORDS

[Upon completion of all thirty-six links. —Ed.]

ŌOKA: After the Romantics, poets have been doomed to live under the spell of sanctified notions of "individuality," "originality," and "genius." These notions lay as cursed burdens upon the consciousness of many poets. "Be original; if not, thou art no more than a poor living cadaver as an artist!" Thus the history of contemporary poetry has produced a throng of poets, isolated, misunderstood and misunderstanding themselves, inevitably autistic, paler than cadavers.

Needless to say, originality is indispensable in making poetry. Nevertheless, it is also imperative for any poet worthy of the name to learn from and even to imitate other great poetry, ancient and modern, and to practice his art in active discourse with it. We learn what originality is only through imitation and exchange with others. That is, we can be original only by connecting with others. In this sense, relations with other poets should be both competitive and cooperative. And I believe the most creative connection, the most stimulating to poetry's vitality, is one that is both. Herein lies the supreme value of *renshi*. This is a form of making poetry which requires us to re-define the notion of originality as a vital energy released through the competitive cooperation among individuals, rather than as something operating within the limited realm of one person's special competence.

Clearly, had I not had the chance to make this *renshi* with three American poets in Hawai'i, I could never have written, by myself, such links as "Shadow for Us All" (9), "This Choice of Death" (13), "As We Wait for the Clear Dawn" (25) and "As All Around Us the Desolate Night Descends" (29). These poems were directly inspired, of course, by the poems of Wing Tek Lum. But at the same time, as I wrote I was always wondering how my link would function and how it would affect the others in the whole work in progress. And it was a source of truly luxurious pleasure to know the other poets were sharing the same feeling.

I wished to express that sense of pleasure in my last link, "The Clear, White Midnight Air" (33), and I was grateful to Wing Tek for providing me with that title. This last poem of mine took the shape it did from the fullness of my joy and my pride in having found in Jean Toyama, Joseph Stanton and Wing Tek Lum true friends living in Hawai'i.

Renshi can also become a form of therapy, a mechanism for liberating one from the autistic prison of the ego, a prison fabricated by the ego itself. Hypnotism is a basic tool of psychotherapy. In our *renshi* we engaged in a surprisingly creative round of group therapy while we were all, I am sure, wide awake. And yet, when I recall our collective psychological state as we made these thirty-six links, I cannot help thinking that we were all indeed in a hypnotic trance of the best sort.

TOYAMA: Although each poem is a discrete entity, I was amazed to see how certain emotions flowed from one to another and ebbed into other shapes. In particular I was delighted by the dark hues that emerged after Makoto's link twenty-one. The "big hole at my back" appeared to create some horror house ride, a dark tunnel into which each of us followed, me chased by a wolf, Joe by some dark memory, and Wing Tek by some oozing slime. Fortunately his "clear dawn" helped us emerge from that hole, and we survived the flood.

Unfortunately I put us in a war, albeit a "good little war," but my partners left the battlefield for other fields, where I found myself under a peach tree. I remembered the most delicious peach I have ever eaten in my life. A *momo*, a Japanese peach. I hope that the reader can sense that beneath the trees not only hunger is being sated.

In my last link I pay an inaudible tribute to Samuel Beckett by trying to imitate his rhythm and tone, while also recounting my experience in *renshi* with my collaborators. Our gathering was an accident, a lucky chance for me. Makoto's, Joe's, and Wing Tek's contributions mark my work, and the energy in their poems, I hope, spark through my own.

I am now veiled with a wispy sadness that this whole process is almost over and that I will no longer be obliged or have the right to intrude into the lives of my fellow poets with a link that will require their response. Nor will I be obligated to respond to their links, a sweet coercion. This is only to underline the usual solitary life of a poet who writes by that inner necessity that makes one write but is at times itself a flaccid need.

Renshi certainly will not replace the poet in his aloneness reacting to life and recharging his world with the inner energy of words. But it does give relief to that silence. Telephones and fax machines are not quiet creatures.

STANTON: I tried to convey in the thirty-fifth poem, "Accidents into Life," my sense of the exciting riskiness of our *renshi*-writing adventure. Re-reading the twists and turns of our collaboration is a kind of roller-coaster ride. By that I mean that despite the leaps and lunges there does seem to be a continuous track. The poems link mechanically to the last line of the previous poem. But there are also subtler turns toward other poems that have gone before. The sequence as a whole has a surprising degree of organic unity for a work by several hands.

To borrow some phrases from one of Makoto's essays, we four writers have "stepped into each other's workshop," developed our *renshi* into a shared "banquet," and found ways to "adapt" and "harmonize" our efforts so that they belong to a common whole. The poems I have contributed to this *renshi* all have a family resemblance to one another and constitute a departure from the kind of writing I have previously done. The requirement of brevity and the corresponding need for imagery that has impact within a brief space constrained me to a certain intensity of focus. Also, the tendency toward the dreamlike, the vividly surrealistic, that developed in my *renshi* poems was probably, at least in part, due to the influence of Makoto's first poem and my reading of a number of his other works. Dreamlike contributions to the *renshi* by Jean and Wing Tek also helped to keep me on that track.

Despite the prevalence of dream in my *renshi* poems, I was also drawn by the influence of certain poems of Wing Tek's to want to write in direct ways about family matters. This influence was not solely due to Wing Tek's contribution to the *renshi*. I have also been affected by the compelling family poems that figure prominently in his *Expounding the Doubtful Points* volume. As I have already explained, my first impulse for "Wiping the Tears from My Eyes" (11) was to write about deaths in my family long ago. Although I did not stick with that impulse, I did finally return myself to childhood in "To Begin" (19) and "A Little War (27).

Jean's influence often led me in the direction of wit and verbal play. Following directly after her in the *renshi* sequence, I was often entranced by her distinctive word choices and her willingness to be humorous from time to time. In addition to "I Am" (15), I would cite "Getting Its Fill" (23) as an example of Jean's wit overflowing into my poem. At least part of what is going on there is that the wolf on Jean's tail is menacing my "silhouetted house," causing that afflicted edifice to throw its hands up in front of its face.

LUM: The limitation on ego referred to in my opening remarks can be a liberating experience; sometimes too much freedom feeds only our selfish desires. Participating in this linkage has forced me to come up with poems I would otherwise never have dreamed of. And looking back I am surprised at what I was able to contribute. I had a lot of blank moments these past few months, though in the very beginning I felt proud that I could churn out my pieces as quickly as my fellow poets. But I got into a big rut around Christmastime and for several weeks could not follow up on "and will not be won" ending Joe's "A Little War" (27). I also got into a dark funk for a while, which I think prompted Makoto to wake me up in poem twenty-nine. Upon reflection, I note that my contributions sometimes turned out quite purple (e.g., poem 8); "It is Only His" (12) on the other hand is one of the better pieces I have written, I think. Reading my fellow poets' contributions as they came over the telecopier one by one was one of the major joys of this collective endeavor. I looked forward to reading their poems as if I were an observer of an ongoing saga. There were many strong images: Joe's moon in the third poem, Makoto's scorpionfish (13), and Jean's wolf on her tail (22). I am grateful to have been a part of the link with them.

Notes on the Poets

WING TEK LUM is a Honolulu businessman and poet. His first collection of poetry, *Expounding the Doubtful Points*, was published by Bamboo Ridge Press in 1987.

MAKOTO ŌOKA is Japan's foremost contemporary poet, President of the Japan P.E.N. Club, and Professor of Japanese Literature at the National University of Fine Arts and Music. He is the author of eighteen volumes of poetry; he has also published plays and film scripts, and has written extensively in the fields of poetics, classical Japanese poetry, and literary and art criticism. He is the recipient of several major awards for both his poetry and literary criticism. His poetry is available in English translation in *A String Around Autumn* (1982), *A Play of Mirrors: Eight Major Poets of Modern Japan* (1987), both from Katydid Books, and *Elegy and Benediction* (Jitsugetsu-kan, 1991). Also in English is a volume of literary criticism, *The Colors of Poetry: Essays on Classic Japanese Verse* (Katydid Books, 1991).

JOSEPH STANTON is Director of the Center for Arts & Humanities at the University of Hawai'i at Mānoa. Recent poems of his have appeared in *Poetry, Poetry East, New York Quarterly, Harvard Review,* and *Yankee.* Several of his Noh-inspired poems are being set to music by composer Byron Yasui. His scholarly interests center around comparative arts, particularly poems inspired by paintings or other works of art. He has recent articles in *Art Criticism, Journal of American Culture,* and *Yearbook of Interdisciplinary Studies in the Fine Arts.* He has published numerous textbooks on literature and language. He is now writing a book on Winslow Homer for James J Kery Publishers.

JEAN YAMASAKI TOYAMA is Professor of French literature and language at the University of Hawai‘i at Mānoa. Her poetry has appeared in an anthology of Asian-American women's art and literature, *The Forbidden Stitch* (Calyx Press, 1989), in journals in Hawai‘i (*Mele*) and England (*Illuminations*), and in Nicaragua's *La Prensa Literaria* and Argentina's *Cormoran y delfín* in Spanish translation. She has also won prizes for her short stories. She has published widely in her scholarly field, most recently co-editing with Nobuko Ochner a volume of comparative studies on language, literature and biography entitled *Literary Relations East and West* (*Literary Studies East and West*, vol. 4, 1990), and a study of Samuel Beckett's trilogy, *Beckett's Game* (Peter Lang, 1991).